MONEY

Compiled by Vijay from the writings of
Sri Aurobindo and the Mother

SRI AUROBINDO SOCIETY
Pondicherry

Yoga in Everyday Life – Booklet Series

1. Meditation
2. Prayer & Japa
3. Yoga
4. Aspiration
5. Surrender & Grace
6. Transformation
7. Illness – Causes & Cure
8. Illness & Perfect Health
9. Sleep & Dreams
10. Food
11. Work
12. Money
13. True Education
14. Education – How to Teach
15. Education – How to Learn
16. Helping Humanity
17. Beauty
18. Truth
19. Occultism
20. Death
21. Rebirth
22. Gods & The Divine
23. Fate & Free-Will
24. Happiness & Peace
25. Aim of Life
26. Attitudes in Life
27. Self-Perfection
28. Perfection of Life
29. Love – Human & Divine
30. True Love

ISBN 81-7060-090-1

First Centenary Edition: 1972
Fourth Edition: 1994
Reprinted in 1997

All Rights Reserved
Writings of Sri Aurobindo and the Mother are copyright
Sri Aurobindo Ashram Trust, Pondicherry
(The excerpts from "White Roses" are copyright Huta)

Published by Sri Aurobindo Society, Pondicherry
Printed in India at Sri Aurobindo Ashram Press, Pondicherry

This is one in a series of thirty booklets published by the Sri Aurobindo Society under the title "Yoga in Everyday Life." Our effort is to bring together, from Sri Aurobindo and the Mother, simple passages with a practical orientation on specific subjects, so that everyone may feel free to choose a book according to his inner need. The topics cover the whole field of human activity, because true spirituality is not the rejection of life but the art of perfecting life.

While the passages from Sri Aurobindo are in the original English, most of the passages from the Mother (selections from her talks and writings) are translations from the original French. We must also bear in mind that the excerpts have been taken out of their original context and that a compilation, in its very nature, is likely to have a personal and subjective approach. A sincere attempt, however, has been made to be faithful to the vision of Sri Aurobindo and the Mother.

We hope these booklets will inspire the readers to go to the complete works and will help them to mould their lives and their enviornments towards an ever greater perfection. The quotations from Sri Aurobindo are prefaced by his symbol and those from the Mother by her symbol.

The Mother's   Sri Aurobindo's

"O TRUTH, COME, MANIFEST."
"आयाहि सत्य आविर्भव"

CONTENTS

Money and Commercialism 1

The Money-Force – Nature and Value 5

Money in Right and Wrong Hands 7

Money – The True Attitude 11

Asceticism and Poverty not our Ideal 18

Business and Spirituality 20

MONEY AND COMMERCIALISM

 But if Science has thus prepared us for an age of wider and deeper culture and if in spite of and even partly by its materialism it has rendered impossible the return of the true materialism, that of the barbarian mentality, it has encouraged more or less indirectly both by its attitude to life and its discoveries another kind of barbarism, – for it can be called by no other name, – that of the industrial, the commercial, the economic age which is now progressing to its culmination and its close. This economic barbarism is essentially that of the vital man who mistakes the vital being for the self and accepts its satisfaction as the first aim of life. The characteristic of Life is desire and the instinct of possession. Just as the physical barbarian makes the excellence of the body and the development of physical force, health and prowess his standard and aim, so the vitalistic or ecomomic barbarian makes the satisfaction of wants and desires and the accumulation of possessions his standard and aim. His ideal man is not the cultured or noble or thoughtful or moral or religious, but the successful man. To arrive, to succeed, to produce, to accumulate, to possess is his existence. The accumulation of wealth and more wealth, the adding of possessions to possessions, opulence, show, pleasure, a cumbrous inartistic luxury, a plethora of conveniences, life devoid of beauty and nobility, religion vulgarised or coldly formalised, politics and government turned into a trade and profession, enjoyment itself made a business, this is commercialism. To the natural unredeemed economic man beauty is a thing otiose or a nuisance, art and poetry a frivolity or an ostentation and a means of advertisement. His idea of civilisation is comfort, his idea of morals social respectability, his idea of politics the encouragement of industry, the opening of markets, exploitation and trade following the flag, his idea of religion at best a pietistic formalism or the satisfaction of certain vitalistic emotions. He values education for its utility in fitting a man for success in a competitive or, it may be, a socialised industrial existence, science for the useful inventions and knowledge, the comforts, conveniences, machinery of production with which it arms him, its power for organisation, regulation, stimulus to production. The opulent plutocrat and the successful mammoth capitalist and organiser of industry are the superman of the commercial age and the true, if often occult rulers of its society.

The essential barbarism of all this is its pursuit of vital success, satisfaction, productiveness, accumulation, possession, enjoyment, comfort, convenience for their own sake. The vital part of the being is an element in the integral human existence as much as the physical part; it has its place but must not exceed its place. A full and well-appointed life is desirable for man living in society, but on condition that it is also a true and beautiful life. Neither the life nor the body exist for their own sake, but as vehicle and instrument of a good higher than their own. They must be subordinated to the superior needs of the mental being, chastened and purified by a greater law of truth, good and beauty before they can take their proper place in the integrality of human perfection. Therefore in a commercial age with its ideal, vulgar and barbarous, of success, vitalistic satisfaction, productiveness and possession the soul of man may linger a while for certain gains and experiences, but cannot permanently rest. If it persisted too long, Life would become clogged and perish of its own plethora or burst in its straining to a gross expansion. Like the too massive Titan it will collapse by its own mass, *mole ruet sua*.

*

 There are two points which resist strongly — all that has to do with politics and all that has to do with money. These are the two points on which it is most difficult to change the human attitude....

As for financial matters, that is, finding a means of exchange and production which is simple — "simple", well, which should be simple, simpler than the primitive system of exchange in which people had to give one thing to get another — something which could in principle be world-wide, universal; this is also altogether indispensable for the simplification of life. Now, with human nature, just the very opposite is happening! The situation is such that it has become almost — intolerable. It has become almost impossible to have the least relation with other countries, and that much-vaunted means of exchange which should have been a simplification has become such a complication that we shall soon reach a deadlock — we are very, very close to being unable to do anything, to being tied up in everything. If one wants the smallest thing from another country, one has to follow such complicated and laborious procedures that in the end one will stay in one's own little corner and be satisfied with the potatoes one can grow in one's garden, without hoping to know anything at all about what is going on and happening elsewhere.

Well, these two points are the most resistant. In the human consciousness this is most subject to the forces of ignorance, inconscience and, I must say, quite generally, ill-will. This is what most refuses all progress and all advance towards the truth; and unfortunately, in every human individual this is also the point of resistance, the point that remains narrowly stupid and refuses to understand anything it is not used to. There it is truly a heroic act to want to take up these things and transform them. Well, we are trying this also, and unless it is done, it will be impossible to change the conditions of the earth.

*

For the last hundred years or so mankind has been suffering from a disease which seems to be spreading more and more and which has reached a climax in our times; it is what we may call "utilitarianism". People and things, circumstances and activities seem to be viewed and appreciated exclusively from this angle. Nothing has any value unless it is useful. Certainly something that is useful is better than something that is not. But first we must agree on what we describe as useful – useful to whom, to what, for what?

For, more and more, the races who consider themselves civilised describe as useful whatever can attract, procure or produce money. Everything is judged and evaluated from a monetary angle. That is what I call utilitarianism. And this disease is highly contagious, for even children are not immune to it.

At an age when they should be dreaming of beauty, greatness and perfection, dreams that may be too sublime for ordinary common sense, but which are nevertheless far superior to this dull good sense, children now dream of money and worry about how to earn it.

So when they think of their studies, they think above all about what can be useful to them, so that later on when they grow up they can earn a lot of money.

And the thing that becomes most important for them is to prepare themselves to pass examinations with success, for with diplomas, certificates and titles they will be able to find good positions and earn a lot of money.

For them study has no other purpose, no other interest.

To learn for the sake of knowledge, to study in order to know the secrets of Nature and life, to educate oneself in order to grow in consciousness, to discipline oneself in order to become master of oneself, to overcome one's weaknesses, incapacities and ignorance, to prepare oneself to advance in life towards a goal that is nobler and vaster, more generous and more true... they hardly give it a thought and consider it all very utopian. The only thing that matters is to be practical, to prepare themselves and learn how to earn money.

THE MONEY-FORCE – NATURE AND VALUE

Money is the visible sign of a universal force, and this force in its manifestation on earth works on the vital and physical planes and is indispensable to the fullness of the outer life. In its origin and its true action it belongs to the Divine. But like other powers of the Divine it is delegated here and in the ignorance of the lower Nature can be usurped for the uses of the ego or held by Asuric influences and perverted to their purpose. This is indeed one of the three forces – power, wealth, sex – that have the strongest attraction for the human ego and the Asura and are most generally misheld and misused by those who retain them. The seekers or keepers of wealth are more often possessed rather than its possessors; few escape entirely a certain distorting influence stamped on it by its long seizure and perversion by the Asura. For this reason most spiritual disciplines insist on a complete self-control, detachment and renunciation of all bondage to wealth and of all personal and egoistic desire for its possession. Some even put a ban on money and riches and proclaim poverty and bareness of life as the only spiritual condition. But this is an error; it leaves the power in the hands of the hostile forces. To reconquer it for the Divine to whom it belongs and use it divinely. for the Divine life is the supramental way for the Sadhaka.

*

You see, when one thinks of money, one thinks of bank-notes or coins or some kind of wealth, some precious things. But this is only the physical expression of a force which may be handled by the vital and which, when possessed and controlled, almost automatically brings along these more material expressions of money. And that is a kind of power. It is a power of attracting certain very material vibrations, which has a capacity for utilisation that increases its strength – which is like the action of physical exercise, you see – it increases its strength through utilisation.

For example, if you have a control over this force – it is a force which, in the vital world, has a colour varying between red, a dark, extremely strong red and a deep gold that's neither bright nor very pale. Well, this force – when it is made to move, to circulate, its strength increases. It is not something one can accumulate and keep without using. It is a force which must always be circulated. For example, people who are misers and accumulate all the money, all the wealth they can attract towards themselves, put this force aside without using its power of movement; and either it escapes or it lies benumbed and loses its strength.

*

First of all, from the financial point of view, the principle on which our action is based is the following: money is not meant to make money. This idea that money must make money is a falsehood and a perversion.

Money is meant to increase the wealth, the prosperity and the productiveness of a group, a country or, better, of the whole earth. Money is a means, a force, a power, and not an end in itself. And like all forces and all powers, it is by movement and circulation that it grows and increases its power, not by accumulation and stagnation.

What we are attempting here is to prove to the world, by giving it a concrete example, that by inner psychological realisation and outer organisation a world can be created where most of the causes of human misery will be abolished.

*

Money is not meant to make money, money is meant to make the earth ready for the advent of the new creation.

*

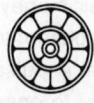

A day shall come when all the wealth of this world, freed at last from the enslavement to the antidivine forces, offers itself spontaneously and fully to the service of the Divine's Work upon earth.

MONEY IN RIGHT AND WRONG HANDS

...The power of money is at present under the influence or in the hands of the forces and beings of the vital world. It is because of this influence that you never see money going in any considerable amount to the cause of Truth. Always it goes astray, because it is in the clutch of the hostile forces and is one of the principal means by which they keep their grip upon the earth. The hold of the hostile forces upon money-power is powerfully, completely and thoroughly organised and to extract anything out of this compact organisation is a most difficult task. Each time that you try to draw a little of this money away from its present custodians, you have to undertake a fierce battle.

And yet one signal victory somewhere over the adverse forces that have the hold upon money would make victory possible simultaneously and automatically at all other points also. If in one place they yielded, all who now feel that they cannot give money to the cause of Truth would suddenly experience a great and intense desire to give. It is not that those rich men who are more or less toys and instruments in the hands of the vital forces are averse to spend; their avarice is awake only when the vital desires and impulses are not touched. For when it is to gratify some desire that they call their own, they spend readily; but when they are called to share their ease and the benefits of their wealth with others, then they find it hard to part with their money. The vital power controlling money is like a guardian who keeps his wealth in a big safe always tightly closed. Each time the people who are in its grasp are asked to part with their money, they put all sorts of careful questions before they will consent to open their purses even a very little way; but if a vital impulse arises in them with its demand, the guardian is happy to open wide the coffer and money flows out freely. Commonly, the vital desires he obeys are connected with the sex impulses, but very often too he yields to the desire for fame and consideration, the desire for food or any other desire that is on the same vital level; whatever does not belong to this category is closely questioned and scrutinised, grudgingly admitted and most often refused help in the end. In those who are slaves of vital beings, the desire for truth and light and spiritual achievement, even if it at all touches them, cannot balance the desire for money. To win money from their hands for the Divine means to fight the devil out of them; you have first to conquer or convert the vital being whom they serve, and it is not an easy task.

*

How can money be reconquered for the Mother?

Ah!... There is a hint here. Three things are interdependent (Sri Aurobindo says here): power, money and sex. I believe the three are interdependent and that all three have to be conquered to be sure of having any one – when you want to conquer one you must have the other two. Unless one has mastered these three things, desire for power, desire for money and desire for sex, one cannot truly possess any of them firmly and surely. What gives so great an importance to money in the world as it is today is not so much money itself, for apart from a few fools who heap up money and are happy because they can heap it up and count it, generally money is desired and acquired for the satisfactions it brings. And this is almost reciprocal: each of these three things not only has its own value in the world of desires, but leans upon the other two. I have related to you that vision, that big black serpent which kept watch over the riches of the world, terrestrial wealth – he demanded the mastery of the sex-impulse. Because, according to certain theories, the very need of power has its end in this satisfaction, and if one mastered that, if one abolished that from human consciousness, much of the need for power and desire for money would disappear automatically. Evidently, these are the three great obstacles in the terrestrial human life and, unless they are conquered, there is scarcely a chance for humanity to change.

*

Money is something one ought not to have until one no longer has desires. When one no longer has any desires, any attachments, when one has a consciousness vast as the earth, then one may have as much money as there is on the earth; it would be very good for everyone. But if one is not like that, all the money one has is like a curse upon him....

It is infinitely more difficult to be good, to be wise, to be intelligent and generous, to be more generous, you follow me, when one is rich than when one is poor. I have known many people in many countries, and the most generous people I have ever met in all the countries, were the poorest. And as soon as the pockets are full, one is caught by a kind of illness, which is a sordid attachment to money. I assure you it is a curse.

So the first thing to do when one has money is to give it. But as it is said that it should not be given without discernment, don't go and give it like those who practise philanthropy, because that fills them with a sense of their own goodness, their generosity and their own importance. You must act in a sattwic way, that is, make the best possible use of it. And so, each one must find in his highest consciousness what the best possible use of the money he has can be. And truly money has no value unless it circulates. For each and every one, money is valuable only when one has spent it....

Wealth is a force – I have already told you this once – a force of Nature; and it should be a means of circulation, a power in movement, as flowing water is a power in movement. It is something which can serve to produce, to organise. It is a convenient means, because in fact it is only a means of making things circulate fully and freely.

This force should be in the hands of those who know how to make the best possible use of it, that is, as I said at the beginning, people who have abolished in themselves or in some way or other got rid of every personal desire and every attachment. To this should be added a vision vast enough to understand the needs of the earth, a knowledge complete enough to know how to organise all these needs and use this force by these means.

If, besides this, these beings have a higher spiritual knowledge, then they can utilise this force to construct gradually upon the earth what will be capable of manifesting the divine Power, Force and Grace. And then this power of money, wealth, this financial force, of which I just said that it was like a curse, would become a supreme blessing for the good of all....

MONEY – THE TRUE ATTITUDE

You must neither turn with an ascetic shrinking from the money power, the means it gives and the objects it brings, nor cherish a rajasic attachment to them or a spirit of enslaving self-indulgence in their gratifications. Regard wealth simply as a power to be won back for the Mother and placed at her service.

All wealth belongs to the Divine and those who hold it are trustees, not possessors. It is with them today, tomorrow it may be elsewhere. All depends on the way they discharge their trust while it is with them, in what spirit, with what consciousness in their use of it, to what purpose.

In your personal use of money look on all you have or get or bring as the Mother's. Make no demand but accept what you receive from her and use it for the purposes for which it is given to you. Be entirely selfless, entirely scrupulous, exact, careful in detail, a good trustee; always consider that it is her possessions and not your own that you are handling. On the other hand, what you receive for her, lay religiously before her; turn nothing to your own or anybody else's purpose.

Do not look up to men because of their riches or allow yourself to be impressed by the show, the power or the influence. When you ask for the Mother, you must feel that it is she who is demanding through you a very little of what belongs to her and the man from whom you ask will be judged by his response.

If you are free from the money-taint but without any ascetic withdrawal, you will have a greater power to command the money for the divine work. Equality of mind, absence of demand and the full dedication of all you possess and receive and all your power of acquisition to the Divine Shakti and her work are the signs of this freedom. Any perturbation of mind with regard to money and its use, any claim, any grudging is a sure index of some imperfection or bondage.

The ideal Sadhaka in this kind is one who if required to live poorly can so live and no sense of want will affect him or interfere with the full inner play of the divine consciousness, and if he is required to live richly, can so live and never for a moment fall into desire or attachment to his wealth or to the things that he uses or servitude to self-indulgence or a weak bondage to the habits that the possession of riches creates. The divine Will is all for him and the divine Ananda.

In the supramental creation the money-force has to be restored to the Divine Power and used for a true and beautiful and harmonious equipment and ordering of a new divinised vital and physical existence in whatever way the Divine Mother herself decides in her creative vision. But first it must be conquered back for her and those will be strongest for the conquest who are in this part of their nature strong and large and free from ego and surrendered without any claim or withholding or hesitation, pure and powerful channels for the Supreme Puissance.

*

(Based on a conversation with Sri Aurobindo)
You said about the forces that control money that two conditions were necessary. First, one must be very calm and must not get disturbed and have no desire for money. Secondly, it requires a bojhāpoḍā *— an understanding — with the universal forces. What is this understanding?*

There are many ways. Even in the case of one man there are different methods, I mean in the yogic sense, which he can follow. First you must put your need before God and ask him to satisfy it; your duty ends there. In that case you need not have any *bojhāpoḍā* — understanding — with the universal forces.

But we look upon money as a power of the Divine, and, as with everything else, we want to conquer it for the Divine in life. Hence, in our case an "understanding" is necessary. As the money-power to-day is in the hands of the hostile forces, naturally, we have to fight them. Whenever they see that you are trying to oust them they will try to thwart your efforts. You have to bring a higher power than these and put them down. First, they try to trick you by offering success, — one can say, by trying to buy you up. If a man falls into that trap then his spiritual future is ruined.

You have really to follow a certain rhythm of the money-power, the rhythm that brings in and the one that throws out money.

Money is given to you in the beginning; then, you have to deserve it. You have to prove that you do not waste it. If you waste it, then you lose your right to it.

What is waste?

Waste is waste. Throwing away money without any order, unorganised expenses without regard to the means of getting money or to the utility of spending. It is not that you have to hoard money. It is there for being spent. But we must spend it in the right way – in a certain order and with an arrangement.

Even the industrial magnates who get money get into that rhythm of which you spoke.

Of course, they do, otherwise they can't get rich. They take it in and then again they throw it out, then it returns and again it is thrown out. That is the reason why they get colossal wealth. These rich people often have no attachment to money, it is the action of the vital force that they enjoy, not their money.

It is a life-movement.

Yes. That was the ideal of the Vaishya as opposed to the Bania – the miser. The Vaishya was the man who could get tremendous wealth and could spend it liberally, could establish the interchange and enter into the rhythm.

*

Sri Aurobindo speaks of "a weak bondage to the habits that the possession of riches creates".

When you are rich and have a lot of money to spend, generally you spend it on things you find pleasant, and you become habituated to these things, attached to these things, and if one day the money is gone, you miss it, you are unhappy, you are miserable and feel all lost because you no longer have what you were in the habit of having. It is a bondage, a weak attachment. He who is quite detached, when he lives in the midst of these things, it is well with him; when these things are gone, it is well also; he is totally indifferent to both. That is the right attitude: when it is there he uses it, when it is not he does without it. And for his inner consciousness this makes no difference. That surprises you, but it is like that.

*

The conflict about money is what might be called a "conflict of ownership", but the truth is that money belongs to no one. This idea of *possessing* money has warped everything. Money should not be a "possession": like power it is a means of action which is given to you, but you must use it according to... what we can call the "will of the Giver", that is, in an impersonal and enlightened way. If you are a good instrument for diffusing and utilising money, then it comes to you, and it comes to you in proportion to your capacity to use it as it is meant to be used. That is the true mechanism.

The true attitude is this: money is a force intended for the work on earth, the work required to prepare the earth to receive and manifest the divine forces, and it – that is, the power of utilising it – must come into the hands of those who have the clearest, most comprehensive and truest vision.

To start with, the first thing (but this is elementary) is not to have the sense of possession – what does it mean, "it is mine"?... Now, I don't quite understand. Why do people want it to belong to them? – so that they can use it as they like and do what they want with it and handle it according to their own conceptions? That's how it is. On the other hand, yes, there are people who like to store it up somewhere... but that is a disease. To be sure of always having some, they hoard it.

But if people understood that one should be like a receiving and transmitting station and that the wider the range (just the opposite of personal), the more impersonal, comprehensive and wide it is, the most force it can hold ("force" that is translated materially: notes and coins). This power to hold is proportional to the capacity to use the money in the best way — "best" in terms of the general progress: the widest vision, the greatest understanding and the most enlightened, exact and true usage, not according to the warped needs of the ego but according to the general need of the earth for its evolution and development. That is to say, the widest vision will have the largest capacity.

Behind all wrong movements, there is a true movement; there is a joy in being able to direct, utilise, organise in such a way that there is a minimum of waste and the maximum of result. It is a very interesting vision to have. And this must be the true side in people who want to accumulate money: it is the capacity to use it on a very large scale. Then, there are those who very much like to have it and spend it; that is something else — they are generous natures, neither regulated nor organised. But the joy of being able to satisfy all *true* needs, all necessities, is good. It is like the joy of changing a sickness into health, a falsehood into truth, a suffering into joy; it is the same thing: to change an artificial and foolish need — which does not correspond to anything natural — into a possibility which becomes something quite natural. So much money is needed to do this or that or the other, so much is needed to arrange this, to repair that, to build this, to organise that — that is good. And I understand that people like to be the channels through which the money goes exactly where it is needed....

Money does not belong to anybody. Money is a collective possession which should be used only by those who have an integral, comprehensive and universal vision. I would add something to that: not only integral and comprehensive, but essentially *true* as well; a vision which can tell the difference between a use which is in accord with the universal progress, and a use which could be termed fanciful. But these are details, for even the mistakes, even, from a certain standpoint, the waste, help the general progress: these are lessons learned the hard way.

*

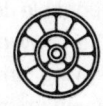

When the idea comes to you: "I want to make the best use of my money" (and the best use, not only from the viewpoint that this gentleman or lady conceives as being useful), well, one can always find out. Generally (there are exceptions), generally these people who have a lot of money put one condition: it must bring them at least some satisfaction. There must be some merit – they give, but they must get something. If they are not business people and do not give their money to gain more, if they are, for example, philanthropists who wish to give money to help humanity make progress, they always wish, more or less consciously (but generally very consciously) they always wish, that it should bring them fame, a kind of satisfaction of their *amour-propre*. They give money for founding a school: the school will bear their name. They build a monument somewhere: it must be mentioned that Mr. So-and-so has donated the money and so on.... There was a time when I was building Golconde; there were people who approached me or sent others to me to say: "I am quite willing to give you so much or so much, but you must place in one of the rooms a marble tablet on which is written: "This room has been built by the gift of Mr. So-

and-so." Then, I said: "I am sorry. I can make marble tablets for you but I'll pave the basement with them!" It is like that.

ASCETICISM AND POVERTY NOT OUR IDEAL

There is, of course, also the ascetic idea which is necessary for many and has its place in the spiritual order. I would myself say that no man can be spiritually complete if he cannot live ascetically or follow a life as bare as the barest anchorite's. Obviously, greed for wealth and money-making has to be absent from his nature as much as greed for food or any other greed and all attachment to these things must be renounced from his consciousness. But I do not regard the ascetic way of living as indispensable to spiritual perfection or as identical with it. There is the way of spiritual self-mastery and the way of spiritual self-giving and surrender to the Divine, abandoning ego and desire even in the midst of action or of any kind of work or all kinds of work demanded from us by the Divine. If it were not so, there would not have been great spiritual men like Janaka or Vidura in India and even there would have been no Krishna or else Krishna would have been not the Lord of Brindavan and Mathura and Dwarka or a prince and warrior or the charioteer of Kurukshetra, but only one more great anchorite. The Indian scriptures and Indian tradition, in the Mahabharata and elsewhere, make room both for the spirituality of the renunciation of life and for the spiritual life of action. One cannot say that one only is the Indian tradition and that acceptance of life and works of all kinds, *sarva karmāṇi*, is un-Indian, European or western and unspiritual.

*

Fling not thy alms abroad everywhere in an ostentation of charity; understand and love where thou helpest. Let thy soul grow within thee.

Help the poor while the poor are with thee; but study also and strive that there may be no poor for thy assistance.

*

The old Indian social ideal demanded of the priest voluntary simplicity of life, purity, learning and the gratuitous instruction of the community, of the prince, war, government, protection of the weak and the giving up of his life in the battlefield, of the merchant, trade, gain and the return of his gains to the community by free giving, of the serf, labour for the rest and material havings. In atonement for his serfhood, it spared him the tax of self-denial, the tax of blood and the tax of his riches.

*

The existence of poverty is the proof of an unjust and ill-organised society, and our public charities are but the first tardy awakening of the conscience of a robber.

*

Valmikie, our ancient epic poet, includes among the signs of a just and enlightened state of society not only universal education, morality and spirituality but this also that there shall be none who is compelled to eat coarse food, none uncrowned and unanointed, or who lives a mean and petty slave of luxuries.

*

The acceptance of poverty is noble and beneficial in a class or an individual, but it becomes fatal and pauperises life of its richness and expansion if it is perversely organised into a general or national ideal.

*

Poverty is no more a necessity of social life than disease of the natural body; false habits of life and an ignorance of our true organisation are ·in both cases the peccant causes of an avoidable disorder.

*

Athens, not Sparta, is the progressive type for mankind. Ancient India with its ideal of vast riches and vast spending was the greatest of nations. Modern India with its trend towards national asceticism has fully become poor in life and sunk into weakness and degradation.

*

Do not dream that when thou hast got rid of material poverty, men will ever so be happy or satisfied or society freed from ills, troubles and problems. This is only the first and lowest necessity. While the soul within remains defectively organised there will always be outward unrest, disorder and revolution.

BUSINESS AND SPIRITUALITY

I may say, however, that I do not regard business as something evil or tainted, any more than it is so regarded in ancient spiritual India. If I did, I would not be able to receive money from X or from those of our disciples who in Bombay trade with East Africa; nor could we then encourage them to go on with their work but would have to tell them to throw it up and attend to their spiritual progress alone. How are we to reconcile X's seeking after spiritual light and his mill? Ought I not to tell him to leave his mill to itself and to the devil and go into some Ashram to meditate? Even if I myself had had the command to do business as I had the command to do politics I would have done it without the least spiritual or moral compunction. All depends on the spirit in which a thing is done, the principles on which it is built and the use to which it is turned. I have done politics and the most violent kind of revolutionary politics, *ghoram karma*, and I have supported war and sent men to it, even though politics is not always or often a very clean occupation nor can war be called a spiritual line of action. But Krishna calls upon Arjuna to carry on war of the most terrible kind and by his example encourage men to do every kind of human work, *sarvakarmāṇi*. Do you contend that Krishna was an unspiritual man and that his advice to Arjuna was mistaken or wrong in principle? Krishna goes further and declares that a man by doing in the right way and in the right spirit the work dictated to him by his fundamental nature, temperament and capacity and according to his and its dharma can move towards the Divine. He validates the function and dharma of the Vaishya as well as of the Brahmin and Kshatriya. It is in his view quite possible for a man to do business and make money and earn profits and yet be a spiritual man, practise Yoga, have an inner life. The Gita is constantly justifying works as a means of spiritual salvation and enjoining a Yoga of Works as well as of Bhakti and Knowledge. Krishna, however, superimposes a higher law also that work must be done without desire, without attachment to any fruit or reward, without any egoistic attitude or motive, as an offering or sacrifice to the Divine. This is the traditional Indian attitude towards these things, that all work can be done if it is done according to the dharma and, if it is rightly done, it does not prevent the approach to the Divine or the access to spiritual knowledge and the spiritual life.

*

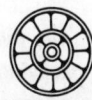

It is said, "One cannot make a heap without making a hole", one cannot enrich oneself without impoverishing someone else. Is this true?

This is not quite correct. If one produces something, instead of an impoverishment it is an enrichment; simply one puts into circulation in the world something else having a value equivalent to that of money. But to say that one cannot make a heap without making a hole is all right for those who speculate, who do business on the Stock Exchange or in finance — there it is true. It is impossible to have a financial success in affairs of pure speculation without its being detrimental to another. But it is limited to this. Otherwise a producer does not make a hole if he heaps up money in exchange for what he produces. Surely there is the question of the value of the production, but if the production is truly an acquisition for the general human wealth, it does not make a hole, it increases this wealth. And in another way, not only in the material field, the same thing holds for art, for literature or science, for any production at all.

When I was doing business (Export-Import), I always had the feeling of robbing my neighbour.

This is living at the expense of others, because one multiplies the middlemen. Naturally, it is perhaps convenient, practical, but from the general point of view, and above all in the way it is practised, it is living at the expense of the producer and the consumers. One becomes an agent, not at all with the idea of rendering service (because there is not one in a million who has this idea), but because it is an easy way of earning money without making any effort. But of course, among the ways of making money without any effort, there are others much worse than that! they are countless.

*

Friends from outside have often asked me this question: "When one is compelled to earn his living, should one just conform to the common code of honesty or should one be still more strict?"

This depends upon the attitude your friend has taken in life. If he wants to be a sadhak, it is indispensable that rules of ordinary morality do not have any value for him. Now, if he is an ordinary man living the ordinary life, it is a purely practical question, isn't it? He must conform to the laws of the country in which he lives to avoid all trouble! But all these things which in ordinary life have a very relative value and can be looked upon with a certain indulgence, change totally the minute one decides to do yoga and enter the divine life. Then, all values change completely; what is honest in ordinary life, is no longer at all honest for you. Besides, there is such a reversal of values that one can no longer use the same ordinary language. If one wants to consecrate oneself to the divine life, one must do it truly, that is, give oneself entirely, no longer do anything for one's own interest, depend exclusively upon the divine Power to which one abandons oneself. Everything changes completely, doesn't it? – everything, everything, it is a reversal. What I have just read from this book applies solely to those who want to do yoga; for others it has no meaning, it is a language which makes no sense, but for those who want to do yoga it is imperative. It is always the same thing in all that we have recently read: one must be careful not to have one foot on one side and the other foot on the other, not to bestride two different boats each following its own course. This is what Sri Aurobindo said: one must not lead a "double life". One must give up one thing or the other – one can't follow both.

This does not mean, however, that one is obliged to get out of the conditions of one's life: it is the inner attitude which must be totally changed. One may do what one is in the habit of doing, but do it with quite a different attitude. I don't say it is necessary to give up everything in life and go away into solitude, to an ashram necessarily, to do yoga. Now, it is true that if one does yoga in the world and in worldly circumstances, it is more difficult, but it is also more complete.

*

If someone has acquired a lot of money by dishonest means, could some of it be asked for the Divine?

Sri Aurobindo has answered this question. He says that money in itself is an impersonal force: the way in which you acquire money concerns you alone personally. It may do you great harm, it may harm others also, but it does not in any way change the nature of the money which is an altogether impersonal force: money has no colour, no taste, no psychological consciousness. It is a force. It is like saying that the air breathed out by a scoundrel is more tainted than that breathed out by an honest man — I don't think so. I think the result is the same. One may for reasons of a practical nature refuse money which has been stolen, but that is for altogether practical reasons, it is not because of divine reasons. This is a purely human idea. One may from a practical point of view say, "Ah! no, the way in which you have acquired this money is disgusting and so I don't want to offer it to the Divine", because one has a human consciousness. But if you take someone (let us suppose the worst) who has killed and acquired money by the murder; if all of a sudden he is seized by terrible scruples and remorse and tells himself, "I have only one thing to do with this money, give it where it can be utilised for the best, in the most impersonal way", it seems to me that this movement is preferable to utilising it for one's own satisfaction. I said that the reasons which could prevent one from receiving ill-gotten money may be reasons of a purely practical kind, but there may also be more profound reasons, of a (I do not want to say moral but) spiritual nature, from the point of view of tapasya; one may tell somebody, "No, you cannot truly acquire merit with this fortune which you have obtained in such a terrible way; what you can do is to restore it", one may feel that a restitution, for instance, will help to make more progress than simply passing the money on to any work whatever. One may see things in this way — one can't make rules. This is what I never stop telling you: it is impossible to make a rule. In every case it is different. But you must not think that the money is affected; money as a terrestrial force is not affected by the way in which it is obtained, that can in no way affect it. Money remains the same, your note remains the same, your piece of gold remains the same, and as it carries its force, its force remains there. It harms only the person who has done wrong, that is evident. Then the question remains: in what state of mind and for what reasons does your dishonest man want to pass on his money to a work he considers divine? Is it as a measure of safety, through prudence or to lay his heart at rest? Evidently this is not a very good motive and it cannot be encouraged, but if he feels a kind of repentance and regret for what he has done and the feeling that there is but one thing to do and that is precisely to deprive himself of what he has wrongly acquired and utilise it for the general good as much as possible, then there is nothing to say against that. One cannot decide in a general way – it depends upon the instance. Only, if I understand well what you mean, if one knows that a man has acquired money by the most unnamable means, obviously, it would not be good to go and *ask* him for money for some divine work, because that would be like "rehabilitating" his way of gaining money. One cannot ask, that is not possible. If, spontaneously, for some reason, he gives it, there is no reason to refuse it. But it is quite impossible to go and ask him for it, because it is as though one legitimised his manner of acquiring money. That makes a great difference.

And generally, in these cases, those who go and ask money from rascals use means of intimidation: they frighten them, not physically but about their future life, about what may happen to them, they give them a fright. It is not very nice. These are procedures one ought not to use.

*

(*Based on an answer by the Mother*)

I have been working for a year in a laboratory where research is being done for the improvement of the quality of the wine and other alcoholic drinks. Where I am, in the South of France, the majority of the population derive their livelihood from the cultivation of the vine and the wine trade. As I am quite sure that alcohol does a great deal of harm to men in general, I do not drink. Therefore, because of my work my conscience is in conflict. I am a sort of conscientious objector and ask myself: 'Can I continue to work and collaborate in this environment'?

Here are a few hints which may help you to find a solution to your problem.

I could tell you, as many an advisor would, that it is up to you alone to solve it, for there is no rule in black and white which can say what you should do. Each case is different, each individual is different, and even for a particular individual the right action, the thing to be done varies with the inner state of consciousness, the stage of development attained.

But it is not likely that this would help you to find a satisfactory solution. Your mind would turn round and round all aspects of the question, all the advices and examples, often contradictory, given by one person or another, without arriving at the knowledge of what ought truly to be done. The only way to extricate yourself is to hand over the problem itself and its solution to the Divine. Let your aspiration be only that of fulfilling at each moment the Divine Will, to do the thing to be done in the way in which it must be done.

"But how to do the Divine Will if I do not know it?" you will ask.

"The problem which presents itself to me is exactly to know it, to know *what* I ought to do. After that all will be easy."

No, the Divine Will is not like the order of a chief which you have merely to execute. What is required is not obedience; it is much more than that — and much more difficult. It is a matter of giving up to the Divine the whole shaping of your life instead of wanting to shape it yourself (even though it be in accordance with the Divine Will). If you can keep intense and constant the aspiration of which I have just spoken and, with this inner attitude, do the work which comes to you, the circumstances themselves will become what they ought to be. If you ought to change your occupation, the circumstances will change and will of themselves lead you to the right occupation, to the work to be done.

It is a difficult attitude, very difficult, for we have been accustomed to act by ourselves, even when we accept an advice or an order. To succeed, an absolute sincerity is necessary, and absence of all vanity, and entire faith and trust in the Divine. This is what the Mother tells me to write in reply to your question. She sends you her blessings.

REFERENCES – MONEY

Booklet
Page

1	SABCL Vol. 15, pp. 72-73	14	MCW Vol. 4, pp. 375-76
3	MCW Vol. 9, pp. 166-67	15	MCW Vol. 13, pp. 275-77
4	MCW Vol. 12, pp. 353-54	17	MCW Vol. 5, pp. 161-62
5	SABCL Vol. 25, pp. 11-12	18a	SABCL Vol. 23, p. 676
6a	MCW Vol. 6, pp. 249-50	b	SABCL Vol. 17, pp. 102-103
b	MCW Vol. 13, p. 154	20	SABCL Vol. 23, pp. 675-76
7a	MCW Vol. 15, p. 53	21	MCW Vol. 4, pp. 376-77
b	MCW Vol. 15, pp. 53-54	22	MCW Vol. 4, pp. 377-78
c	MCW Vol. 3, pp. 45-46	23	MCW Vol. 4, pp. 379-81
9	MCW Vol. 4, pp. 381-82	26	Sri Aurobindo Circle (No. 7), pp. 161-62
10	MCW Vol. 7, pp. 54-56		
11	SABCL Vol. 25, pp. 12-14		
13	Evening Talks (ed. 1982), pp. 336-38		

N.B. Abbreviations: SABCL – Sri Aurobindo Birth Centenary Library
MCW – Mother's Collected Works

The quotation in the last line of the Introduction is from 'White Roses'.